# Motherland

# Motherland

Poems by

Heather Nelson

© 2025 Heather Nelson. All rights reserved.
This material may not be reproduced in any form, published,
reprinted, recorded, performed, broadcast,
rewritten, or redistributed without
the explicit permission of Heather Nelson.
All such actions are strictly prohibited by law.

Cover design by Shay Culligan
Cover image by Felipe Paes on Pexels
Author photo by Kristen Emack

ISBN: 978-1-63980-745-1

Kelsay Books
502 South 1040 East, A-119
American Fork, Utah 84003
Kelsaybooks.com

*To my family, who inspired* Motherland *and give me love and purpose every day, and especially to my husband, Larry Kolodney, whose unflagging support and generosity over the years have enabled me to do my work as a writer.*

# Acknowledgments

Grateful acknowledgment is made to the following journals in which these poems first appeared, sometimes in different versions.

*The Compassion Anthology:* "Prodigal"
*Constellations:* "Father's Day"
*Cult Magazine:* "Addicted to a Sense of Urgency"
*Ekphrastic Review:* "Half-Naked Woman with Coin," "Shade"
*Free State Review:* "Sophia's Away at Ballet Intensive"
*Hags On Fire:* "Virtual Accountability Group"
*I-70 Review:* "Basement Quarantine"
*Lily Poetry Review:* "Whale Watching"
*Lyrical Somerville*: "Fresh Pond Fallen," "Fifty on the Floodplain"
*Main Street Rag:* "Demeter at the Plough & Stars"
*Nixes Mate Review:* "Gay Head Beach"
*Orenburg Mountain Poetry Journal:* "Number One Bus," "Self Portrait"
*Panoply:* "Erica Ventricosa (Italian Heather)"
*Quinobequin Review:* "Perimenopausal Aubade," "Post Apocalypse Under the Charles"
*Spilling Cocoa Over Martin Amis:* "Mindfulness + Beauty"
*Spoon River Review:* "We Jazz July," "Midlife Almanac"

"The Leaning Tower," "Resilience," and "Two Sisters" were featured on Boston Area Small Press and Poetry Scene's *The Sunday Poet Series.*

# Content

| | |
|---|---|
| How to Fall | 15 |
| Whale Watching | 16 |
| Waning Crescent | 17 |
| I Try to Outrun Vulnerability | 18 |
| Self Portrait | 19 |
| Longitudinal Survey | 20 |
| Father's Day | 21 |
| My Last Fuckable Day | 22 |
| off-brand flower | 23 |
| The Mom Shop | 24 |
| 4$^{th}$ of July | 25 |
| Demeter at the Plough & Stars | 27 |
| At Manuel Antonio Park on My 50$^{th}$ Birthday | 29 |
| Almost Midnight | 30 |
| Post Apocalypse Under the Charles | 31 |
| Springtime Comedy | 32 |
| Girls & Sex | 33 |
| Midlife Almanac | 34 |
| Cold Valentine | 35 |
| We Jazz July | 36 |
| On the Pulse of a COVID Winter Morning | 37 |
| War Poem | 39 |
| Shade | 40 |
| Crimes Against God (a Cambridge Poem) | 41 |
| Prodigal (for Jahar Tsarnaev) | 42 |
| Half-Naked Woman with a Coin | 44 |
| Two Hotel Rooms | 45 |
| Motherland | 46 |
| Lactation Diary | 48 |
| Sophia's Away at Ballet Intensive | 49 |
| Blushing Hydrangeas | 50 |
| Resilience | 51 |
| The Leaning Tower | 52 |
| Fifty on the Floodplain | 54 |

| | |
|---|---:|
| Last Family Excursion Before Quarantine | 55 |
| Fresh Pond, Fallen | 56 |
| Walden, revisited | 57 |
| Recruited on Zoom by the Black Panther Party | 58 |
| When Driving the Atmospheric River, from San Francisco to Santa Cruz | 59 |
| The Restless Leg (Quarantine Dream) | 60 |
| On the Lincoln Road | 61 |
| Erica Ventricosa (Italian Heather) | 62 |
| Two Sisters | 63 |
| Addicted to a Sense of Urgency | 64 |
| Virtual Accountability Group | 65 |
| Calgon Take Me Away | 66 |
| Flower Talk | 67 |
| Fifty-two and a half | 68 |
| Basement Quarantine | 69 |
| Owen Heads Back to School | 70 |
| The Winter We Met | 71 |
| From My Window | 72 |
| Substitute | 73 |
| Turning Fifty-One | 74 |
| Teaching Hawthorne at Belmont High | 75 |
| Ode to Teacher Shoes | 76 |
| Mindfulness + Beauty | 77 |
| A Poem Is Not a Trust Fall | 78 |
| Perimenopausal Aubade | 79 |
| August at the Ekphrastic Cafe | 80 |
| The Whale Watch, Four Years Later | 81 |
| Gay Head Beach | 82 |
| Local Warming | 83 |
| Number One Bus | 84 |

*Live the questions now.
Perhaps then, someday far in the future,
you will gradually, without even noticing it,
live your way into the answer.*

—Rainer Maria Rilke

# How to Fall

Let your pallor plumply proclaim
that you'll be cushioned as you fall.
Pad yourself in purple Patagonia.
Gird yourself in gray Irish wool.

When you fall, make sure to get spread
and splayed like a Christmas tree
thrown to the curb, holiday past,
your pallor no longer ornamental.

Crash despite the cash
in your dark Coach bag, despite
the kind advice you offer, the kind of advice
you wanted, but never had.

# Whale Watching

Provincetown curls
with longing: I stick
to the boat's insides.
My gaze rakes and smooths
the ocean's surface
like a Zen Garden within
an equally-enormous sky,
framed by frantic gulls,
gorging on the cold.

When I emerge I'm restless,
straining against the rail
until a small, silken sudden
teal saturation bursts open
and a slapping tail absconds
with my words, leaving a barb
in my gut. The sea will hold
the weight I cannot carry.

# Waning Crescent

lounging just above
the roof-line, grey mackerel
sky streaming towards
sunset along the river,
view framed by smokestacks.

The moon moves like salmon
striving forward, tumbling down
blindly seeking
an apex, its opaque arc lifts
for a moment, points up.

# I Try to Outrun Vulnerability

*Freedom is frightening,*
said Toni this morning.
Or did she say *art?*

I let myself feel
the wind and the grit of the city—
that's what cities are for.

I let myself see
the sun slanting towards setting in mid-afternoon—
that's what winter is for.

I stroll Osaka with the Makioka sisters
at just the right pace—
we trace life's trajectory together.

# Self Portrait

Watch me stretch my supple frame, ample mass, awful expanse. I fill the entire bedside mirror, floor to ceiling. Each morning my borders shift as I acquire more territory. I crawl into the belly of Central Square, a beast that contains heat compactly. I eat all I find, prowling the autumn blocks looking for marrow to suck out of the tiny yellow leaves on the sidewalk. Outside the YMCA, my belly speaks in a voice that's deep, rumbling sonorous underfoot like the subway passing beneath the swimming pool, beneath the undergrads, the yoga instructors, the spin doctors, this year's models, sucking everyone down.

# Longitudinal Survey

Were the promises of Emancipation fulfilled?
A seat at the ACLU dinner goes for $500 a plate.

Should I step back or should I step in?
When I bend, the blood in my body courses with corrosive rage.

Why am I attracted to younger men?
When we meet him on the train, the young man's attention renews our relevance

What should I avoid?
Falling asleep, driving in dreams.

What bird has time for feelings?
Replace them with loneliness, a skyline silhouette.

Which way to SimCity?
Through any poem within a five-year radius.

Did you have a hard day?
In truth, I'm as soft as a pillow.

What's the best seat in your car?
The passenger seat is optimal—they control the music.

# Father's Day

*after "Crossing Brooklyn Ferry" by Walt Whitman*

The month of June is mapped except for the
third Sunday, it's a yawning gap of time
a question mark on my calendar, will
the father who is missing ever come?
Or is that space too amply filled, though
too many fathers is no improvement. I
link the divorces to my birth—that derailment, I can't stop
talking about it. My cluttered nomenclature is here
to stay, it's where I live. I speak of Dad today
then of birth father and step-father and
know they'll continue to jostle in my dreams tonight.

We're short on love and slack on duty, then what
could ever bring us together? I left home for good, is
there still a reason to see each other two hours a year? Would it
be it worth it to continue to exchange gifts, then
what follow up, how to fill the time between
the times we briefly meet, as if only distance divided us?

## My Last Fuckable Day

The canvas of May is practically blank.
I turn the calendar to Arches National Park,
but the page itself is naked: no meetings, no appointments,
no theater, no music, no book group, no poetry.
I leave those blank squares and wander.
Heading straight down the row I fall in
to another week of folding laundry.

This spring I miss the chance to breathe
the lilacs deeply, the chance to resent the metaphors
they always evoke, to hate every blossom
for its derisive youthfulness and fertility. We
could go walking again together, these coy mean girls
and me. I could fill my canoe with flowers,
drift a good long while . . .

This gigantic canvas will take centuries to fill.

## off-brand flower

In the Nineties, off-brand was our thing—
that's how we liked to live.
That's why Kurt made Courtney
return the Lexus, keep the Volvo.
We wanted to be boxy, but serviceable.

Driving through Freeport, Maine, I won't stop.
I'm that averse to LL Bean, skirting the styles I hope to avoid.
Arriving back in Cambridge,
a receiving line of rusty mums and purple pansies
reminds me that I'm boxed, in my very own brand.

# The Mom Shop

It's a stretch to say it opens at six, call it seven, time for coffee and a look at the street, gray and also rising. At seven o'clock, I turn time's handle, set the mill of the day in motion. The mom shop's still open, I dutifully turn the sign each morning, waiting for someone to serve. Owen, my only customer, has finished his oatmeal, left the bowl in the sink, and headed to high school. Many items are out of stock. The shelves are sparse, their offerings paltry. Someone should take the time to shove the best items forward. The wall clock ticks and drags, the wall calendar flashes garish October. Nine to three is make-work, walks and washing, setting the stage for a reenactment of the early years, when the mom shop was at capacity, serving three kids at a time. I love the part of the day when I spot my last (and only) customer rounding the corner through the shop window. I see him before he sees me, am at the door before he can open it.

# 4th of July

*Bread of bitterness,* I mutter as I stalk through the living room, swooping down on a dirty coffee mug, as I drift into the kitchen, a black bean squelching under my bare foot. It's what I'm gnawing on. Stale bourgeois bitterness, like the 2 day old baguette, like the stain on my leather sectional where I lie each afternoon, staring out at the basketball hoop, thinking of my oldest son, who's mostly gone. Because it's a holiday, after all, I set out to buy picnic supplies. Beyond my row of brick houses is an abandoned lot, then a parking lot, then Prospect Street, too dangerous for children to cross. Catty corner at 5 Temple Place is an impromptu parlor, set up right on the sidewalk, filled with: mattresses, chairs, people, weed; fenced in by Blue Bikes, temporarily free. Back home, I pack canvas tote bags with snacks and jackets for our excursion. At 10 PM, I head out towards the river with my husband and youngest son to watch the fireworks. In the small enclosure by the Greek Orthodox Church, someone sleeps on the ground, covered in a light blanket. By the cell phone store on Mass Ave, a young woman in a black dress dances, facing the glass. *It's a new era in cannabis* quips Owen, our recent 8th-grade graduate, as we walk through Graffiti Alley. Little Donkey's windows are open to the street and its barstools are full, cocktails and tapas. *Whose bullets are we dodging tonight?* The question stays unspoken in my head, our feet walk ahead, seek prime real estate for fireworks viewing, a few feet of concrete on the ledge by the bridge. DPW trucks blockade the area, giving us a feeling we're protected, a feeling we're all together, perhaps at summer camp. Memorial Drive is closed and every few minutes a kid on a bike comes whooping down the underpass, voice echoing raucous and jubilant. After the grand finale, the crowd leaves together, filling the street, ambling along with our chairs and our strollers, our skateboards and our coolers. Turning the corner onto the block before our house, there's a tall man pushing a shopping cart full of bags and wearing a grinning monkey mask on the back of his head. He turns around and asks me how I'm doing tonight. I say I'm fine and he asks me, in a serious tone, *would you like me to sing a song for you?*

# Demeter at the Plough & Stars

*after Robert Frost*

Aging we grow second Natures,
rounder and deeper than our first.
It's perverse, this thirst for green
that keeps our barstools spinning. Is
anyone still looking for their gold?

Demeter's a mom, knows what waits for her,
but not what she is missing, that's the hardest.
part of heading home, afternoon's resolute hue
of returning, chiming children to
assemble, to gather, and to hold.

Demeter's AWOL at the bar, knows it'll be just her
alone in the row, arriving too early,
too made-up, her late summer leaf's
gilded to lure a stranger, but who will pluck a
ripe fruit, if they're looking for a flower?

Here's her playbook: I hate to say this but,
I'm the only
woman here, so
given you're a man, I've got an
idea, not much of a plan, for spending this hour.

I'll ask the questions, then
in the lowered light, as you leaf
through the menu and talk subsides,
I'll head for the Ladies Room, I'll decide to
leave you, sliding your drink over the sticky table leaf.

I'm not an ingenue or a tramp, so
if we play at East of Eden
I'll be the rebel who sank
into madness born of impatience to
expunge early grief.

Demeter's got an hour or so,
he has from now till dawn.
That's the way it goes
he's sure to let her down.
Yet the thought burns and lingers, to
be naked as the day.

He sports black linen, she has nothing
to line his pockets, she's all out of gold.
Demeter's strands are silver, and even he can
see, if she was asked, she would stay.

# At Manuel Antonio Park on My 50<sup>th</sup> Birthday

At nine in the morning, I'm already hot
as I start down the Monkey Trail.
Where the paths divide, I see a cactus.
I want to test the pain, so I touch it, pressing
the pad of my index finger against the point until
it almost hurts. I remind myself that I'm alone
because I asked to be. The cicadas are my company,
they never stop talking. Their sound hovers
over my head, brushes my shoulder, rattles me.
On the bamboo bridge, I look up, notice the clacking dark
green fronds of the palm. Idly, the wind rustles. I wait
together with my nagging fear of erasure
until I can move again.

## Almost Midnight

After we make love
I'm alone but not-
not rushing to wash,
not sleepy, not tense, unworried
by kids still up and nearby.

I lie contented
on my back sinking softly
fully flat, relaxed
more alert than usual
wakeful without midnight fear.

Light travels across
our ceiling, fleet and frantic
sirens, blue then red,
flicker outside our window
but we stay here together.

Humming, then quiet
my center calms. Ears open-
street sounds are sharp and
sweet. I don't need to know, but
still whisper, *can you hear it?*

# Post Apocalypse Under the Charles

When Cambridge becomes Tokyo, its trains and houses
will overflow and we will all be wet.
Young or old, we won't find shelter in luxury towers.
We will cluster close together under sunken trees.

Phosphorescent night
will overtake morning. Unlikely lovers,
fragile strangers, will float, approach, and touch.

I'll stop wishing for my eighteenth birthday,
stop looking out for my lover drifting by.
I'll know him when he arrives wearing his aqua shirt.
Fear, no longer my lap dog, will leave its window seat.

# Springtime Comedy

nostalgia for what
wasn't another April
blooms behind a fence

nose and tongue at once
lilac's synesthesia
returns lost gardens

my other body
isn't pretty, isn't pink
is hidden, endures

my face, morning sun
my age: the weight of summer's
cornucopia

springtime comedy:
high mimesis, fallen from
youth, cloaked in flowers

# Girls & Sex

*after Peggy Orenstein*

Each summer I walk
the marsh with Sophia. We both
are older, her hair,
longer, her legs,
summer's shell opening.

Marsh smell hits us: hot,
rank, deeply satisfying.
My legs spread slightly,
relaxed like the rivulet—
sun-baked and teeming with life.

When she gets older,
she'll learn to lie low as grass,
won't need to stand so straight.
She'll bend with pleasure, be full,
at last, won't give up so fast.

# Midlife Almanac

There's no index, but I can find my spot
the way grades are decided late at night.
Just toss the papers down the steps, wherever
the book falls open is where I will be.

The first page is June. I take the family camping.
The water's smell and depth daunt me and I wait
by the lake's edge for my own life-preserver,
tight and ungainly. I'm the annual beginner.

My paddling is game, but painfully clumsy.
Any eighteen-year-old could intuit what
I must learn carefully and with chagrin.
Twist, then dip in deep, push and keep pushing.

My left arm, weak and recalcitrant.
My eyes, shallow roots of the lilies

The dark lake rocks my boat. First gentle,
then brisk slaps. It warns against the dark green
sheets of surface. *If you sleep, even for a moment,
the deep water will be your bed.*

# Cold Valentine

February in Copley Square is concurrently
loving, careless and cruel. Morning serves beauty
with disgust: milky white clouds in plump, pendulous
dollops, clotted cream in a turquoise soupy sky.

A bag lunch will do for us teachers
to eat while walking in a brisk wind
past a woman asking for more cash
so she can go to Starbucks.

At the last bell, sun ignites the school doors,
red cellophane light on pudding stone.
Candy wrappers blow around my sensible shoes.
Men head home dutifully carrying perfunctory flowers.

There's a backup on the Green Line steps, everyone single file
stepping around a man leaning on his elbow, eating a burger,
coat hanging open, eyes blank. In an attempt at etiquette,
I say *take care,* smile stiff and false as I pass.

# We Jazz July

Their Instagram upends my almanac. The kids can't be bothered looking that far ahead. While I am fiddling with my forecast, at nine and fourteen, they are filtering the future. I help my daughter with her backlit pose. She steps into Renoir's evening fields, which fit her perfectly. I snap some covert selfies, but find there is no magic angle—only more or less flattering light. Ruefully, I choose black and white for my backdrop and dispatch my youthful aspirations. Blanche Du Bois was thirty when she asked for softer light. She lacked the rude truths of children, their kindness in holding us to the mirror.

# On the Pulse of a COVID Winter Morning

*But seek no haven in my shadow.
I will give you no hiding place down here.*
     —Maya Angelou


*I'm going for a walk,* I shout up the stairs
to the kids with their earbuds in.

I'm already tired, just standing up
before long johns and wool socks,
before snow boots and masks.

The house tells me there's more to do
but when I pass the mirror, I look away.

Carl Barron Plaza is bleak, it's only me
and the others who have nowhere else to be.
I'm distressed, I walk faster,
until I reach the icy footbridge.

The Charles River tells me it's nothing personal.
It reminds me that I haven't been cold
long enough. On the riverbank are shoes,
jackets and plates piled up by a fence.
Under the steps is a plastic shelter.

*I'm no Master of War,* I posit
huffing up the steps, one foot at a time.
*I'm a busy woman, check my calendar.*
When I get to the top, I'm heading back.

*It's January 2021,* the water calls out,
*time to stand on the rock!*

Do I have to? The river pretends
not to hear my complaint, knows I'd take
a ride home if I could, virtue be damned.
It waits for me to see, there's not another way.

# War Poem

My colonoscopy memoir: *Behind the Brown Curtain*
My immodest rage at obscurity: reminiscent of Putin.
Putin's got issues too, same shit writ large:
who comes first, who's in charge?
My little soldiers rise petulant every morning,
demanding attention despite the warnings.
How many heads need to go on a pike,
before they admit that I've always been right?
My dossier's a testament to my slide,
down Maslow's Pyramid of Needs, the ego-side.
Concession sets the crosshairs of my aggression
Forced altruism can't engender compassion
A militant Madame Bovary, when push comes to shove,
I demand more recognition, just a little more love.
I've been bourgeois since thirty, but I'm always hungry.
How can I be this well-fed and still angry?
A shark circling the tank,
I'm obsessed with my rank.
A washed-up imposter,
I've been put out to pasture.
Brooding at home,
I chew brigadier bones.
Bare chested on horseback I ride through my city
avenging all slights, no matter how petty.

# Shade

*after Kerry James Marshall*


I have no name for the look in your eyes—
blackness is the last thing I'll mention

and then only in terms of ebony and obsidian,
in terms of interiors and privileged pornography.

I see nothing but ice-cream in the pockets
housed outside your shirt. Nothing but pistachio,
dripping with lavender, flowing into a bowl of vanilla.

Your ear I'll call a nautilus, your hair threads of blood—
red woven tightly into your texture, circling the nipple, smudging
the lips.

Your weary phrenology, I read as a novel
you remain invisible, named after my fear.

To keep on looking tests my mettle—your lifted shirt looks like a .
noose.

Your back remains hidden—seeded with scars?

You'd hate me if you knew what I hope for.

Turn around and let me see

the tree of absolution.

# Crimes Against God (a Cambridge Poem)

1. Thou shalt never allow hot water to run freely.

2. Thou shalt not call thy personal trainer from the bistro.

3. God hates the audible chewer.

4. Heed the bedroom door—that it not be left open, even a crack.

5. Ask not that God call you, when she prefers to text.

6. Forever cease retweeting.

7. Pay thee more heed to the overlay zone, than to the man laying on the pavement.

8. Shun not density, but gastropubs.

9. Avoid all claims to have lived in the neighborhood, back when it was real.

10. God doesn't love your recycling, is not pleased by your humble brag.

# Prodigal (for Jahar Tsarnaev)

A remarkable conjunction—
in dreams where a boy is lost
you are too,
on a freeway
far-afield,
bent on a six-o-clock
assignation with another
city, in a parallel April.
The week of the bombing
I dallied with Wordsworth,
basked in Romantic shadow,
peered through digitized
keyholes, at the Gothic cast
apprehension shed upon
the gritty, the striving, the open
face of the Cambridge we'd left behind.
My son cowered
under the duvet,
under slate and stone,
as cameras raced down
his streets, past the schoolyard
past the rug store,
past huddled friends,
he cowered
under the tarp,
trapped by the river,
he cowered with you,
Jahar.
From London to Reykjavik,
and on into Boston,
my dreams were turbulent
full of certainty that I'd lost a boy,
but whose?

Which boys were safe,
lips slack with sleep,
pillows damp with hair
stuck to their cheeks?
Which boys were bleeding,
who was hidden,
which boys could I reach?
Back home the talk is
all of loss, vocal tremors,
everyone shaken, everyone looking
back over their shoulders
for a catch in time
when safe seemed possible.

# Half-Naked Woman with a Coin

*after Jacob Adriaensz Backer*

The view is simple:
a whore in cerulean.
I'm not looking
at you, but asking
you to look
where my eyes are pointing:
first at my breasts,
then to the coin in my hand.

Make yourself comfortable
you won't be listening,
my mouth does the talking.
Look—it's approachable, just slightly
open between teeth barely visible
you'll see a supplicant bit of tongue
glistening within.

My left side, you'll avoid
it's draped deep in the sheen
of dropsy folds soon fallen.
You'll not see what I mean
to keep hidden, under budding
breasts, pushing up like soft pigeons.

# Two Hotel Rooms

I.
In my family's hotel room, there has to be space
for everyone to squeeze between the bedside table
and the shaded side-street view. In our hotel room,
there must be towels for all, body and hand, they must
reappear come late afternoon, the bed again anonymous.
I need to sleep on the side near the bathroom. Knowing
myself, I'll trip over odd angles in the night, waking
the children who are sure to mention that I snore,
sure to imitate me in the morning.


II.
When I stay alone in a hotel room,
a rare event, I am tempted not to leave
the room because I love being alone,
far above the honking. Instead I take
a picture of the street below the window,
drawing back the sheer drapes, letting in
the opaque light of a big city night.
In my hotel room, my hand rests softly
on my stomach, then my thigh—
a solitary tryst, thirteen stories high.

# Motherland

My grocery cart's overflowing, but resentment
keeps me rolling down the aisles, composing my manifesto:
*We mothers should rally!* First we'll spill the organic milk,
then we'll smash the seedless grapes. Why not smash
the Whole Foods marketplace, with its odious agreed-upon doors?

*Smash the shopping!*
*Smash the providing!*
But keep the power that comes with buying?
Keep the secret snacking, on shrimp and aioli?
I sit in the car, irresolute with my groceries as it grows dark.

As far as the night is concerned, I can stay
or go, it's indifferent. But without boundaries,
there is no home. If I'm out too long
my family will wonder where I am. They will try
to find me, will know that I want to be found.

Motherly love is
a form of Stockholm syndrome.
Every inch of me is available, my body
occupied, my arms always open,
working around the clock for love.

They follow me wherever I go, my family
is the delicate net against which my day
strains and rebounds, is the cage in which I am hidden.
At night I lock the bedroom and bathroom doors
to be sure my desires go unnoticed

Come six a.m., once again, my alarm insists:
*Not one step back!*
*You've already agreed to this.*

# Lactation Diary

Furled in the dark, curled on the floor, it's better here. I won't try to get up. We lay on the futon, she and I, gaze through the bars on the window with its view of the flat black garage top, with its view of vines creeping across brick. Why try to sleep when the gas alarm might go off, wailing its complaint: waves of methane wafting from the diaper bucket. I use cloth diapers, thick cotton ones ordered online with cute plastic covers, snap-shut, no pins. Rinse in the toilet, yellow green, breast milk in, liquid shit out: wash, rest, repeat. The whole house smells like a defeated barnyard. We lie on our sides, she and I, rise early for another change.

# Sophia's Away at Ballet Intensive

This morning the mirror over her dresser shows only leaf shadows and dappled light through curtains covered with grey and blue birds. She's been away for a month, and her room is untouched. I hesitate in the doorway, knowing that my sewing scissors are in there somewhere, under half empty bottles of papaya lotion and a pile of unmatched socks. The shaggy black pony on a blond stick quips *hey sexy lady,* eyes me from his post in the corner. The gargantuan Easter rabbit from her Jewish grandfather leans back on the pillow, plumply complacent. Her closet door stays open—to close it would be to hide something from myself. Inside, I see a cluster of defunct pointe shoes, ten pale pink years hanging over the bar. On her wall are Renoir girls, flushed and gilt-framed, huddling together over their book. I leave without finding the scissors, without even looking for them.

## Blushing Hydrangeas

When I was the maiden in the ode,
the arcade was indoors. Quarters went
further then, August gobbled up
the plump clusters, her youthful food.
Today I linger in the arbor
in the wide shade of grape leaves
tantalized by the fruit
dangled for other lips.
Mouths open, blue blossoms wait
for the bait, perhaps a country lad
in a blouse of flax, lute hanging lax
eyes upcast: *it's happening at last.*
Every throw is always the first.
Every day relates to our birth.

# Resilience

On the slim wooden shaft of the women's room key is a query, in black Sharpie. *Do you identify as female?* Literal me, I take all questions seriously, I examine the evidence. The swelling prow of my chest as I thread my way between the coffee shop tables certainly broadcasts a woman's body. As I resume my scone, I look out across the tables at all the other solitudes. Is what they see female? I'm not shopping, I'm not dieting, I'm not waxing. I'm not waiting to be asked. I'm feeding my hunger. I live in this soft and solid house, we're incorporated, this body and I. I'm 49 and full of questions and desire. As we age, does sex fade or intensify? If my gender's fluid, could it overflow and lap at the feet of the beautiful barista boys? That would be hot, but it wouldn't be pretty. Everyone likes to look, but no one really wants to be touched. Midlife is a second childhood, equally turbulent, but less endearing. If we're flirting, it's with ourselves, stretching in front of our mirrors.

# The Leaning Tower

is climbed by appointment—
timed clusters of travelers wind into queues,
shuffling along the edge
of 4:30's scorching shadow.

I am searching for Sophia
when a dark-garbed guard turns my head
with a sharp bark: *Watch your son!*
My blond boy as always is climbing the rails.

I spot her at last—far off
on the grass, behind the Pomodoro statue,
where at 4 p.m., she practiced her shaky
walk-over, dark hair sweeping the ground.

Like an umber fan, hair hid
her burning face, her trembling legs,
the trace of amused scorn at the corner
of her older brother's mouth.

Still waiting, I'm wishing for that morning,
a return to the wall where they all
walked abreast, two boys and a girl,
tramping together along Lucca's rim.

Truthfully there was morning
fighting too, over three bottles of
water, bought just for the bathroom,
spilled struggling over who gets whose first.

Lunch served us a respite under the cover
of a wide canopy, I had enough room
for seven wines poured by the owner's daughter
whose red hair wound across the label of the Rosato.

Our family runs toward noir,
thick brow and olive skin,
sister and big brother twine, arms wrestling,
each boasting a greater darkness.

## Fifty on the Floodplain

That's not me you see
on a hot July morning
just shy of fifty
on what should be a work day
walking by the B.U. Bridge.

Five years ago there
was soccer duty, looking
for a rabbit with
the boy, living in a book
everyone could understand.

Today my purpose
is undecipherable
but clearly I'm here
corporal and blowsy as
the day lilies, that visible.

This is not my street
anymore, only traffic
lights mark my corner—
red, green, then all flat water.
I'm scrambling for higher ground.

It's crowded up here.
We're all naked except for
our life vests, what's left?
Only what we can carry
toward the shifting horizon.

# Last Family Excursion Before Quarantine

I encourage Owen to kick a tree on our walk.
Because he is so angry, he won't do it.
I kick the tree instead. It doesn't flinch—just takes it.
A broad sugar maple, I've learned, can sustain
many taps without injury. If there were a maple god
would she give me more than I could carry?
Would she think like an Audubon volunteer,
earnest and cheery in the early March field
rehearsing as fresh what she's known forever:
the roots, the sap, the buds?

# Fresh Pond, Fallen

I'm sharply reminded
by seven jays harping
the golf course blues
from the fronds of the willow,
that trees, too, have needs.

Furthermore, bittersweet
should not be allowed
to climb so brilliantly high,
taunting the earnest native
gardener with the insouciant
faces of Mandarin orange,
shining with menace.

I'd tend to my hunger if it weren't
always there, its reminder jockeying
for my attention with my husband's voice,
thrown like a stone in the water.

Denial takes practice, my eyes sip
the cordial of berries left for cardinals,
drain the plump green milkweed pods
to the last draught, like absinthe.

# Walden, revisited

Sherman, shall we meet at Walden Pond? You'll have to leave early to hop a boxcar, I'll race you along the tracks. Even if we arrive at more or less the same time, trudging the pond's perimeter, you're bound to remember that Thoreau burned these woods, while I admire his disdain for clothes.

I am by rights a dreamer. Without so much as a by-your-leave, I pluck the Indian figure from your book and send him flying through *La Strada,* dream logic liberation. My eyes snap open in time to catch your skeptical glance. I try to smooth things over with lecture hall snippets—*nature—as landscape*—but before I can finish, your back says it all—a solid wall of contempt.

We meet again that night, somewhere between the worlds. I pull in late to our date at the crossroads, with heated seats and lumbar support. My hair is windswept, your skin is weathered. My road is seamless, yours sutured. My ride zipless, yours fucked. Our eyes meet, and lock. Before we can move, we'll both have to put something down.

# Recruited on Zoom by the Black Panther Party

*after Emory Douglas*

I'm drawn to the central figure,
and she is drawn to me.
Her gaze is direct, I try to stroll past her.
She turns her head, watches me go.

Her gaze inscrutable, I fall
into her eyes, plummet until we reach
the charcoal dark bottom together.

Her chin tilts up the way the boys
greet each other—
*come with?*

She displays her ribcage, her heart,
her arteries pulse visibly
on her shirt like a sash
flung across her chest.

Pink stripes burst out of her back—
they are spokes, and she is the hub.
The pink is psychedelic, her scent
is purple haze.

I want to dance with the crowd
in chaotic unison, a musical herd.

The set of her lips is amused—
she's seen my type before. She's ready
to paint me with a giant brush—pink stripe
running down my center.

# When Driving the Atmospheric River, from San Francisco to Santa Cruz

Keep moving through the fog
fingers brushing your roof.
Stop peering over the ledge,
to see who's gone down.
Best not to stop in your old lover's town.
Better pass by Pacifica,
and his message of late:
*it's been so long since '88.*
Avoid wondering if he's still ripped.
Avoid scanning the surf for his board.
Return safely to your dream of a strong arm
pulling you out of the roiling waves.
Stop looking towards the edge-
keep your eyes on the right white line.

# The Restless Leg (Quarantine Dream)

Last night I dreamed only for a little while,
but in that time I was certain
that I couldn't go home.

I planned a safe voyage, assumed
my mother would have me, wondered
*will she hug me?*

I didn't want to fly there.
I didn't want to change my dreams.
I didn't want what's wantable.

My restless leg is always
visiting and revisiting.
It wants me to choose
my own ending.

# On the Lincoln Road

Channeling Alexie
on the Lincoln Road
meadows flush with tiger lilies
I ask myself:

what invisible hand
shook the cloth of the land,
scattering hummocks of corn and squash,
tidying the pastoral table?

Whose hand moves the pieces
of this Gropius game board
marshals applejack sentries
together to guard
Thoreau's working retreat?

Will our hands raise the edge
of these patterned fields
releasing a noisy contest
of the dissonant
undead?

I roll up the window
slide down the Lincoln Road
on Fellini's fantastic flume,
but not before I catch a glimpse
of Sherman riding beside me
on the dragon's tongue
unfurled.

# Erica Ventricosa (Italian Heather)

The literature of Italy makes me want
more than one name. I'd like to pass for Sicilian.
It's early afternoon on the plaza, only the pizza shops
are open and only the tourists are out.

I'm writing new Italian literature over the old.
I locate my fantasies in places that have their own
stories, graft my wishes onto on the side
of a Vesuvius from which I never have to run.
My literature of Italy has Aperol spritzers
on every page, boar ragu each afternoon.

My Italian opus is florid, just like me
heated and greedy, menopausal,
its languid harbor seen from the sea.

# Two Sisters

Kate and Eliza were two sisters well-met, arch and iconic, late '80s vintage—a typical Richard acquisition. Richard kept shop when the Square was still real, al fresco at Au Bon Pain. Shoulder-to-shoulder with the Chess Master, he sat mixing colors—a splash of kelly green on a wide swath of ball-park mustard yellow. Kate's tresses are luxuriant, her expression skeptical—one plump purple brow permanently raised. Eliza smirks at my feminine conceits, thrusts forward in the frame—*you want some of this?* The two sisters step down from their pedestal, bid farewell to the Silent Bride. Her gig was stationary, theirs dynamic, choosing to watch over us. These Iron Maidens are our minders, unavoidable but solicitous. We are remarkably successful squatters. They are our unswerving guardians, the lady golems of our block.

# Addicted to a Sense of Urgency

*He said,*
He hurried to see her, but when he arrived it was six months too
 early.
He stood under her window, but she refused to open it.
He thought he would try again when he was richer.
He thought he would try again tomorrow, but this time bring an
 umbrella.
He hurried to see her, but so did everyone.
He hurried like it was his own idea, when the line was already two
 blocks long.
He hurried because he loved the feeling of hurrying.
He walked around the block 10 times, but the clock only turned 10
 minutes.
How to keep up a lover's pace?
Run backwards?
Refuse to rise from the pavement?
Nail himself down?

*She said,*
It takes at least six months for them to lose their insincerity.
How long will it take for me to lose my sincerity?
Maybe I already have, I just sound like I haven't.
When I'm angry, the truth just seeps out.
Repression is bad for the digestion, I'd like to shout.
My heart races every afternoon as if I'd heard
a gunshot on my street, but what's there is
just dissonance, cacophony, a jar full of marbles
with nothing to hold them. My executive mind
has already stored each task: by category, by space, by time
then left her desk. Empty portraits run this show,
mine among them.

# Virtual Accountability Group

*I spoke first, I'm sorry, I spoke again,* stumbling over my words. I never wait long enough because I want: an acrostic, a separate apartment, a book of my own.

I know a great shortcut-a wrinkle in time: skip the center. COVID-19 dumped me at the tail-end of middle age.

I object —*the ceiling on my life is lower, I'm sitting on the ground.* I protest—*there's gravel in my shoe, dust in my mouth, my fifty second spring is lost.*

*Step back, stop comparing your loss to that of the young.*
*Your years are all fungible now.*

Why leave the house? Because I can, because a small sailboat might arrive at the door one morning to take me away from my room, my husband, my children, this life.

At home nothing's wrong, but nothing is exactly right. Everyone's remote, wanting more control. I stand outside closed doors, waiting, not listening.

My virtual accountability group knows exactly where my money should go. Nevertheless, I keep showing up the same way every day, against the same background.

## Calgon Take Me Away

Turn on the faucets
release my escapist
tears, let me weep with relief.

Sweep me out of the bathroom
where I'm awake and alone
on a wave of bubble-bath.

Play melancholy
songs, pull up tears
when I want them most.

I need a tear-jerker
to make my face crumple
to dislodge the lump in my throat.

It's best to avoid touching
or trying to touch. It's best
not to want so much.

Bubble baths open painful doors
to my childhood, demand
that I soldier on.

I'd rather conjure
imagined loss, missed connections
what I'm missing.

It's less disappointing
if I stop imagining
next time, the long embrace.

# Flower Talk

Early April always walks
around the same block.
Each year the same small signs appear
as new, fresh fodder for fallacies.

The scilla seem bemused
by my recurring illusions:
*Remember how we spoke last year?*
*Now we're talking about spring, again?*

Last year's cherry blossom frisson
won't make me young again, pink petals land
indifferently on my browning hair. Carrying on
is such a god awful small affair.

Spring flowers mirror
each other
they're the voyeurs
of my aging
of my youth,
of my life
read consecutively.

# Fifty-two and a half

I am charged, this August of my life, not to bypass
the crow. I must note
where he lands in the moist dark mud
of the shaded riverbed. Chipmunks
scramble its chocolate brown borders
and robins, more than once,
flit across my path to remind me that one red leaf
stands out among the green masses.

The red-winged blackbird won't show himself,
but the crow calls over his shoulder:
*It may be dull, it may be somber, but it's your job.*
To be as sober and attentive as I was at 51,
in the suburbs as well as the jungle.
To mark the seasons slow and close,
their color and their movement.

# Basement Quarantine

I sit out back as darkness creeps over the patio,
waiting for his motion to trigger the light.
Instead, there's a noise in the front—
the VW pulling up to the bumper of my car.
I hustle around in time to catch Nathan
heading up the front steps, key in hand.
*You're not going through the house are you?*

Nathan's not really part of the house anymore
even when he's here. His room is full of dirty clothes.
If you quarantine at home, you should be a hermit.
It doesn't bother him the way it bothers me.
The house is just a box.
*Mom, be consistent in what's not allowed.*

At 18 I lived in my room, waiting to leave.
I was through with running up the stairs and slamming my door.
The slam meant *come ask me why I'm mad*
but no one ever came.
This house knows me better, it holds
the room in which I fall asleep and all
the windows that show me morning.

On the last day of August, Nathan is gone.
Patio light off, front door locked, towels all in the laundry.
I thought it would be a relief, dropping him off in Middletown,
beech trees shading the first acorns on the ground.
Instead I'm alone in the living room, Miles Davis on the stereo,
folding laundry on the sectional, counting the weeks
until his return.

# Owen Heads Back to School

These mornings I'm walking behind Owen, all the way to second grade. My lagging is purposeful, it feeds his momentum, propels his Razor scooter around the park's perimeter. First to the corner is a certainty, of which he never tires.

Owen's head is back-lit by September's sun, his steps slowed by its amber filter. A verging wind shuffles the haystack of his hair, slides down the sharp quiver that splits his shoulder blades.

Following, I take note of the last honeysuckle, the first crab apple, the rusty edging of the upper leaves. Like me, the trees are lush and avoidant, flailing against the season.

# The Winter We Met

Mt Auburn is fanged from Athens to Banks Street. Nape bent as offering, I step with care into the boot soles of other winter's walkers, skidding on their memories. Surrounded by porous embankments, I wear snow's coat of ash. I am studded with rubble. Seen in the side-mirror of a half-buried car, I am a fractured sphinx sporting snaky locks gone sepia. Februus snatches me straight from the street, wants me for his own. He plunges me into a dry ice mikvah, lifts and holds me for a frozen moment, then leaves without closing the door. I'm free to go, but for my task of rubbing other frozen lives against my own. I'm snow's queen. Puzzled-questions form, then stall, fogged with breath. By the small window I'll stay, waiting for March to find me. *Over here! On the floor!*

# From My Window

As a girl, I would find,
looking out the window, I'd been left behind.

From my window it seemed the the whole block shared my dream
we would hear the truck coming then run for ice cream.

The dream season starts with a trip to the lake,
will those senior boys invite me to partake?

At last cold beers, shared towels on sand
sun seeps through my eyelids, I'm finally tan.

Can I quick step-back across the age line?
Throw the car in reverse, lurch back in time?

Can't I swim just as well as before?
I used to turn heads—I ought to turn more.

# Substitute

I'm not as blond as you are—an authentic piece of straw,
gold as a tale that bears repeating.

You're not as green as I am—an alien shade,
wild and invasive as late summer.

I'm not as thin as you are—wired for sound,
embedded even under the floor.

You're not as young as I am—my heat
fills the room, we'll need to open a window.

I'm not as attuned as you are—four minutes
of my dissonance stumbles over your silence.

You're not as desperate as I am, my earnestness
unbearable, like a love-struck teen.

I'm not as cool as you are—pale with poise,
unrehearsed, already graceful.

You're not as hot as I am—flushed with exertion,
flattened by love.

# Turning Fifty-One

It's a February morning on Inman Street:
iced and salted, bramble edged, cast in pewter.

Last year's birthday was festive and fraught, a Costa Rican
reckoning. This year, I picture the days ahead as empty morning
blocks.

I took the day off to walk alone, the long way home,
to imagine the questions no one knows to ask me:

What's in the hand behind my back?
What do I keep warm, deep in my coat?

I am always being followed on these walks.
I walk slowly, knowing it's my hunger.

# Teaching Hawthorne at Belmont High

The Scarlet Letter
pulses like a heart worn on
my substitute sleeve.

Long legs lope in
all ears are corded to the waist
all eyes on me.

My black sweater, my red skirt
colored physiognomy
far-too-close reading.

Red signals anger
or arousal or both:
sainted slut, boy toy.

Flat Stanley:
a global paper-doll, like-
wise me, classroom moll.

Flash to game time, I'm
lifted on testosterone's
strangely-sticky crest.

Hester is hot, and
the others are not, so they
put her on the stocks.

Jail is a black flower.
Students toss bouquets
I stoop to gather.

## Ode to Teacher Shoes

Suede black, low-slung boots,
bought with thoughts of urban outings
now scuffed and salted
shuffling through slush to the T,
kicked off at home by the door.

What drudgery,
to hold my old trudging feet,
to work in common
with their pedestrian peers
on daily sidewalks.

My swollen, shackled shoes
walk each day like Oedipus:
blind to where home is,
forgetting the earth below them,
bound to their own path.

# Mindfulness + Beauty

It's the second Monday after I quit, five
years is epic, I can rest for a bit.
Indulgences are strategic when shown the exit,
I'll get no sympathy if I wear a target.
On the morning of my pedi,
I can't find my glasses, can't seem to get ready
I take a Xanax, try to keep my gaze steady,
get behind the wheel, text goodbye to the family.
At the Beauty Spa I extend my swollen foot
to the technician who kneels at her habitual spot.
She's tired and practical, I'm deep in thought, my
relaxation imperative seems overwrought.
I leave with toes the color of wine
not blissed out or bitter, I'll settle for fine.

# A Poem Is Not a Trust Fall

I'm not a leaver, I haven't lost it
my unbearable lightness hides in the closet.
It stays married to my fears—
we get heavier very year.
When I write, it's my fight,
a chance to slip into the night
to meet Robert Johnson as he might
have sold his soul to play legendary guitar,
be waiting at the crossroads in his car.
If my desk were a portal to a Brooklyn beer hall,
if I were taking a cruise to Turkey this fall,
then at six o'clock I'm sure I'd be able
to put tacos for five on the table.
To face down the self-judgment I hear every night—
as the voice of my longing could also be right.

# Perimenopausal Aubade

Spring shudders awake like a city.
The crows cry: *4:30, 4:30!*

I glide in and out of sleep, inhaling
warm morning, exhaling pink noise.

I fluff my pillow up and flip it over,
releasing the cool night air.

I lift my hair in one sheet,
soothing the nape of my neck.

Entombed as a pharaoh, I stare
at the digital clock face projected on the ceiling.

I don't have to get up to guess what's going on:
the maple is scattering whirly-gigs.

A skein of pollen is settling on my windshield.
The street sweepers swish and flash.

Soon I'll drive through Harvard Square playing Joni Mitchell.
She'll sing "Help Me," and I'll feel free as any co-ed.

I'll drive right out of town, grey hair blown back
windows rolled down.

# August at the Ekphrastic Cafe

By the time I arrive at the museum,
I'm late, and pay dearly for parking.
Every entrance is the wrong one. Moreover,
I'm not a member.

Of the two cafes, I'm more familiar
with the one shaded by the Chihuly tree.
No one's there and I long for a pause—
for a cool glass of wine with that grass green
freshness.

Renoir and Degas are already at the cafe,
settled and sanguine, chatting easily about their friendship,
how it all began. I sit down with a clatter,
dig for a pen, fail to find it. Why am I so hot?
Might be lack of water, might be that I'm never as fresh,
never as pressed, as the sleeve and the collar across the table.

My notes too are scrambled, I must look as I'm writing,
must describe my ugly hands. There's an angry rash
between my fingers, blue-ink smudging their tips. Veins bulge
over the back of my hands, anxiety crosshatches my palms.
The fist grasping my borrowed pen makes an angry face
contorted with effort to locate a memory of real light in my
childhood.

# The Whale Watch, Four Years Later

Here again with the family on Macmillan Wharf,
threading the queue of drag queens. Declining all shows,

I lug jackets, backpacks and my uncertainty
down the corrugated plank.

I've excised the longing from my last poem,
but I'm still defiant, insisting that the peninsula is my finger.

I'm still impatient too, unable to rest my eyes,
raking the waves for the same teal bubble.

This time, I retreat to the leeward side,
savoring the shade and the scent of nachos.

I struggle to make my case: type firmly into my phone,
*Today I am the figurehead.*

I hold the camera high, reverse the view.
This selfie will show them: my hair is still golden—my eyes are
also blue.

In the background, I spot my Sophia, alone at the prow,
dark hair blown back, farther out than I've ever been.

The bleak horizon sweeps away intent,
first blue, then grey, then blue again.

At last the ocean looks back, with a diffusely tender gaze,
reminds me that the evening light loves only me.

# Gay Head Beach

Even the Earth's face is a man's face,
creased and indifferent to the spectacle
created by his nakedness.
Exhaustion and striving vie in Earth's profile
gouged red, striped white, slathered brown and grey.
*Grim-visaged war,* between origin and appetite,
carves his features. His face is proud
in a grim way, beautiful in the bitter sense.
Flayed by wind, he weathers
repeated blows. To each lash and lull
of the pewter waves capped with pyrite,
he offers again his cheek of clay,
tenders his hostility with resignation.

# Local Warming

February hedges full of hidden
sparrows twitter brightly
warm a patch of concrete,
crack through the ice.
Snowdrops emerge, furtively,
too soon. I love them furtively
because the time is wrong,
because they are my secret.
I was once a teacher, now I shop
like everyone else. Instead of writing,
I take yoga. Rather than emptying
myself of want, I envision sirloin steak, marbled with fat.
Once, I fought age, now I slide
into fifty-six. Once again,
I close my eyes, try to return
to where I am right now.

# Number One Bus

The rain is coming down harder than it was
at three o'clock on Newbury Street.
I'm wearing Fluevogs, watching the boys
in Vans ride skateboards on the sidewalks,
stepping around the woman who sleeps
on the ground, glad to have a destination.
A summons to what I'm not sure, but I'm glad
to work where families feel safe
sending their children, even if cranes loom
on the waterfront and post-post-modern boxes
jiggle like Jenga towers on the skyline.
Even when dark clouds mass over the river,
I feel fine, because when I arrive in Cambridge,
I meet Whitney out on the wet sidewalk,
and we talk, about wanting work, and finding it.

# About the Author

Heather Nelson has been a student of poetry since college, where she developed her thesis project under the guidance of CD Wright and Peter Gizzi at Brown University in 1991.

After a break, she returned to writing in 2011 and has since been published in *Ekphrastic Review, Lily Poetry Review, Nixes Mate, Spoon River Review,* and many other publications. Heather leads a local free-write group, runs workshops at Grub Street, and plans events for Boston Book Festival's Litcrawl and other community writing events. Heather is already working on her next book of poetry.

www.ingramcontent.com/pod-product-compliance
Lightning Source LLC
Chambersburg PA
CBHW070938160426
43193CB00011B/1729